A RIDE IN EZEKIEL'S WHEEL

A STUDY OF THE FOUR FACES

ANNELLA WHITEHEAD

AGNES I NUMER

ILLUSTRATED BY

SHARALEE CUTHBERT

A Ride in Ezekiel's Wheel: A Study of the Four Faces

Paperback ISBN: 978-1-955759-47-2

eBook ISBN: 978-1-955759-48-9

Unless otherwise indicated, all Scripture quotations are taken from the Holy Bible, King James Version - Public Domain.

Scripture quotations marked (Wuest) were taken from The New Testament: An Expanded Translation (Wuest) translated by Kenneth S. Wuest. Copyright © 1961 by Wm. B. Eerdmans Publishing Co., Grand Rapids, Michigan.

Authors:

Rev. Agnes I. Numer "The Revelation of Jesus Christ"

Rev. Annella Whitehead "A Ride in Ezekiel's Wheel: A Study of the Four Faces"

Cover Art: Sharalee Cuthbert

Illustrations by: Sharalee Cuthbert

Teresa Skinner Publishers

Special Thanks:

To my Mom Grace and my sisters Sharalee, Carey and Melissa, for your love and support and allowing me to be away from you.

Rev. Agnes I. Numer for seeing in me the finished product and imparting Isaiah 58.

Rev. Teresa Skinner for our friendship and teaching me to "ride".

Al and Chas Carvel your love and the encouragement to do the study.

Veronica Sanchez, your friendship and prayers.

"I planted the seed. Apollos watered it, but it was God Who kept it growing." 1 Corinthians 3:6-8 (NLV)

CONTENTS

INTRODUCTION

The late founder of All Nations International, Rev. Agnes I. Numer, often taught on the vision of Ezekiel's Wheel. This vision is a beautiful description and revelation about **how to move with God.** It took many sessions before I finally understood and had a personal revelation of this incredible concept.

Thus began my study on the four Gospels searching for all the attributes needed to function as a servant, as a son, a man, and as a priest.

The Vision of Ezekiel's Wheel exemplifies a call to move with the Spirit of the Lord to accomplish His plan and purpose on the earth.

In this study, we will compare each face of Ezekiel's Wheel - the Ox, the Eagle, the Man and the Lion, - to the four Gospels. Although Jesus' character has many more than four facets, we will focus on the four found in Ezekiel Chapters 1, 2, 3.

What type of lives do we live? Do we live as as Servants of God (the Ox), Sons of God (the Eagle), or as Brothers of Jesus (the Man)? Do we even know **who we are** and that we can live by our God given heritage of the Lion of the tribe of Judah?

As you use this study may you feel propelled to allow God to remove those issues that prevent you from coming into His fullness and add to you what is lacking, that by His Spirit **you might be able to hear, see and respond to the moving of the Spirit of God.** And together you may flow with Him fully and see His Kingdom come.

Please enjoy the study and open your heart to experience the incredible journey of moving with God in Ezekiel's Wheel.

Ezekiel 1:12 "And they went every one straight forward: whither the spirit was to go, they went; and they turned not when they went."

- Annella Whitehead

REVELATION OF JESUS CHRIST

PRAYER

Father, we thank You for the revelation of Jesus Christ. We thank You, Lord, that You're coming again very soon. Lord, You have so much to give us. You have so much to share with us. Drop by impartation into our hearts the vision that we may run by the Spirit of the living God. Thank You, Lord, for what You have for us by Your Spirit and in Your Name. Mighty God, we thank You and we ask You now Lord, to reveal Yourself to us that we may arise and go forth. Realizing the purpose that You've given us this revelation – that the Lord Jesus Christ shall arise in us, and You shall send us forth by the Spirit of God. Send us by the fullness of the Father in the fullness of time, to the ends of the earth, that we may see and behold the glory of the Lord. Thank You, Jesus. We praise You for this. In Your wonderful Name we ask this. Amen.

I. THE REVELATION OF JESUS CHRIST IN US

The Lord's been speaking to me about Ezekiel. If you want a revelation of Jesus Christ open your hearts to receive it, as the Lord gives it to you through Ezekiel 1.

One time just before I moved to this house, the Lord gave me Ezekiel 1, 2, and 3. This was my training ground. Very mighty was the Word of the Lord and it changed my life. He changed it greatly through these chapters. Ezekiel 1 is the Revelation of Jesus Christ. It is Jesus Christ in us, in all His power and in all His glory. This chapter tells His whole story – when He went to heaven and when He was on earth. It's very wonderful. I'm going to share it with you through His Word.

EZEKIEL 1

> *1 Now it came to pass in the thirtieth year, in the fourth month, in the fifth day of the month, as I was among the captives by the river of Chebar, that the heavens were opened, and I saw visions of God. 2 In the fifth day of the month, which was the fifth year of king Jehoiachin's captivity, 3 The word of the Lord came expressly unto Ezekiel the priest, the son of Buzi, in the land of the Chaldeans by the river Chebar; and the hand of the Lord was there upon him. 4 And I looked, and, behold, a whirlwind came out of the north, a great cloud, and a fire infolding itself, and a*

brightness was about it, and out of the midst thereof as the colour of amber, out of the midst of the fire.

5 Also out of the midst thereof came the likeness of four living creatures. And this was their appearance; they had the likeness of a man. 6 And every one had four faces, and every one had four wings. 7 And their feet were straight feet; and the sole of their feet was like the sole of a calf's foot: and they sparkled like the colour of burnished brass. 8 And they had the hands of a man under their wings on their four sides; and they four had their faces and their wings. 9 Their wings were joined one to another; they turned not when they went; they went every one straight forward. 10 As for the likeness of their faces, they four had the face of a man, and the face of a lion, on the right side: and they four had the face of an ox on the left side; they four also had the face of an eagle. 11 Thus were their faces: and their wings were stretched upward; two wings of every one were joined one to another, and two covered their bodies.

12 And they went every one straight forward: whither the spirit was to go, they went; and they turned not when they went. 13 As for the likeness of the living creatures, their appearance was like burning coals of fire, and like the appearance of lamps: it went up and

down among the living creatures; and the fire was bright, and out of the fire went forth lightning. 14 And the living creatures ran and returned as the appearance of a flash of lightning. 15 Now as I beheld the living creatures, behold one wheel upon the earth by the living creatures, with his four faces.

16 The appearance of the wheels and their work was like unto the colour of a beryl: and they four had one likeness: and their appearance and their work was as it were a wheel in the middle of a wheel. 17 When they went, they went upon their four sides: and they turned not when they went. 18 As for their rings, they were so high that they were dreadful; and their rings were full of eyes round about them four. 19 And when the living creatures went, the wheels went by them: and when the living creatures were lifted up from the earth, the wheels were lifted up.

20 Whithersoever the spirit was to go, they went, thither was their spirit to go; and the wheels were lifted up over against them: for the spirit of the living creature was in the wheels. 21 When those went, these went; and when those stood, these stood; and when those were lifted up from the earth, the wheels were lifted up over against them: for the spirit of the living creature was in the wheels. 22 And the likeness of the firmament upon the heads of the living creature was as the colour of the terrible crystal, stretched forth over their heads above. 23 And under the firmament were their wings straight, the one toward the other: every one had two, which covered on this side, and every one had two, which covered on that side, their bodies. 24 And when they went, I heard the noise of their wings, like the noise of great waters, as the voice of the Almighty, the voice of speech, as the noise of an host: when they stood, they let down their wings.

25 And there was a voice from the firmament that was over their heads, when they stood, and had let down their wings. 26 And above the firmament that was over their heads was the likeness of a throne, as the appearance of a sapphire stone: and upon the likeness of the throne was the likeness as the appearance of a man above upon it. 27 And I saw as the colour of amber, as the appearance of fire round about within it, from the appearance of his loins even upward, and from the appearance of his loins even downward, I saw as it were the appearance of fire, and it had brightness round about. 28 As the appearance of the bow that is in the cloud in the day of rain, so was the appearance of the brightness round about. This was the appearance of the likeness of the glory of the Lord. And when I

saw it, I fell upon my face, and I heard a
voice of one that spake.

EZEKIEL 1:1-28

EZEKIEL 2

*1 And he said unto me, Son of man, stand upon
thy feet, and I will speak unto thee. 2 And the
spirit entered into me when he spake unto me,
and set me upon my feet, that I heard him
that spake unto me. 3 And he said unto me,
Son of man, I send thee to the children of
Israel, to a rebellious nation that hath rebelled
against me: they and their fathers have
transgressed against me, even unto this
very day.
4 For they are impudent children and stiffhearted.
I do send thee unto them; and thou shalt say
unto them, Thus saith the Lord God. 5 And
they, whether they will hear, or whether they
will forbear, (for they are a rebellious house,)
yet shall know that there hath been a prophet
among them.*

EZEKIEL 2:1-5

II. KING, SERVANT, SON OF MAN, SON OF GOD

Jesus revealed Himself to Ezekiel who was one of God's major prophets in the land during the time of captivity. Even though Ezekiel was a prophet, it didn't mean he was going to escape captivity. **He sat among Israel as a captive.**

Ezekiel could not minister properly; He could not go to the Jewish people until he personally had the revelation of Jesus Christ. I'm sure he felt like he needed to do something, but it was hopeless without the Spirit of the Lord. **We must first have the revelation of Jesus Christ.** So here is this great prophet of God, sitting by the river Chebar in captivity, with a stubborn and rebellious people who did not want to hear from God and did not want to do what God wanted them to do. He's telling about a whirlwind that came out of the north and a great cloud and fire enfolding itself with a brightness that was around about it, out of the midst thereof as the colour of amber.

Then came the "likeness of four living creatures."

Now, remember, this was written in Ezekiel's day. This was not written after Jesus came - it was written before Jesus came. This was when He wasn't yet a man, but He was the Son of God.

> *5 Also out of the midst thereof came the likeness of four living creatures. And this was their appearance; they had the likeness of a man. 6 And every one had four faces, and every one had four wings. 7 And their feet were straight*

feet; and the sole of their feet was like the sole
of a calf's foot: and they sparkled like the
colour of burnished brass.

EZEKIEL 1:5-7

When you looked at the four living creatures, they had an appearance of a man. The four faces of the four creatures are Christ – Christ Jesus, the servant; Christ Jesus, the Son of Man; Christ Jesus, the Son of God; Christ Jesus, the King. Christ Jesus, bringing forth His body today in the revelation of Himself – Jesus, the Lion of the tribe of Judah; Jesus, the servant; Jesus, the Son of Man; Jesus, the Son of God.

The Gospel of Matthew portrays Jesus as the Lion of the tribe of Judah for the Jews. The Gospel of Mark portrays Jesus as a Servant, an ox. The Gospel of Luke portrays Him as a man, the Son of Man. The Gospel of John portrays Him as an Eagle, the Son of God. Here is the completeness of Christ, on the earth, with the Word of God and with the purpose of God. The Lord brings them together and these creatures represent Jesus in full authority – King, Servant, Son of Man, Son of God – all things complete.

Jesus showed through these scriptures the five fold ministry that He had given to man. Ezekiel saw the hands of a man, these hands represent the hands of man. This was the work, the gifts, and the ministry of the Holy Spirit among the people. The gifts are given to bring the body of Christ into perfection. After the perfect one comes forth, then, the seven-fold spirit of God is going to take the place of the gifts.

The revelation was of Jesus. This is the ministry of Jesus Christ. They had straight feet, they had a purpose - they had a plan. Jesus has a purpose and a plan here in the revelation of Himself. The work that Jesus did when He walked the earth was done by the Son of Man... it was not done by the Son of God.

Remember what happened to Him when He was baptized in water? The Spirit of the Lord came upon Jesus. The Father acknowledged and the people recognized that Jesus was God's Son. He's shown here with a purpose, with a plan.

He was also known as Jesus, the Son of Man. The Father is the big wheel, Jesus is the little wheel, and **we are in Jesus.** Christ in man, man in Christ – the Father, the Son and us.

The eyes in the rim round about it are the seven spirits of God. We're in the middle of it with Jesus, with the gifts, with the ministry and the fullness of Jesus Christ. Something was happening to Ezekiel; he was receiving the revelation of Jesus Christ. The Spirit lifted Ezekiel and something began to happen. Out of this great wheel, the rings around it were full of eyes. The Spirit of the Lord, the Spirit of wisdom, the Spirit of knowledge, the Spirit of understanding, the Spirit of counsel, the Spirit of might and the Spirit of the fear of the Lord. **All at once this wheel began to move,** and it had the appearance of a wheel within a wheel. **As the Spirit began to move, it came to the throne of God and it came back to earth again.**

They had two wings that covered their body. Remember those four faces? They are the character, the nature, of Jesus Christ. He clothed them with true humility. The wings covered them, and they were not visible except for their faces. They were not exalted, but the appearance was the appearance of a man – that man is Jesus Christ, the Son of God, the Son of Man, the Servant, the King of kings and the Lord of lords.

As He brings us into this relationship with Him, there is **not going to be anything in you and I except Jesus.** We'll be clothed in Him, filled with Him, filled with His kingdom and filled with His glory.

As we allow Him to change our life, **we're going to ride on the high places of the earth.** I don't think we ought to waste any time, do you? Jesus wants everyone of us to be like He is. He paid the full price for us, and we need to enter in, and stop being stubborn, stop being rebellious. He wants to use us with the Spirit of the Lord in us, so that we can proclaim this Gospel of the Kingdom to the ends of the earth. It's not a dream, it's a reality. **No one is eligible to ride in this wheel unless they have permitted God to totally train them by the Spirit of the Lord.** There is no one sneaking in – no free rides. We all have to ride by the Spirit of the Lord. There is no halfway. There is no, "I'll do it my way," if you want to ride by the Spirit of the Lord and in His Wheel - you'll do it God's way.

He's giving us a mighty revelation of Jesus Christ and His work as He walked the earth. They rejected Him, but nevertheless He's the King of kings and the Lord of lords. They rejected Him because He was a servant, but, nevertheless, He is still servant to man. "He sits at the right hand of the Father ever making intercession for us." **We have to become a servant to Him.** We have to allow Him to take our life and move through us in the manner He chooses. **If we do not become a servant, we won't have a place with him.** If we don't allow His Spirit to move in us, we miss what He has for us. I'm not saying He doesn't want us to be intelligent. He is the greatest intelligence of all. I prefer personally to let Him be my intelligence. I prefer personally to let His wisdom be my wisdom. I prefer that His understanding and His knowledge be my understanding and knowledge, and His Spirit to have charge of me.

This is what He was doing for Ezekiel: He was preparing him for a special revelation of Jesus Christ. Not only to use him in that day, but for this day – for the revelation of Jesus Christ. The gifts are given here, the ministries are given here. The hands, the ministries, they call them the five-fold ministries. They're all represented here in Ezekiel 1. Everything about Jesus Christ as the man was given here to Ezekiel so that He could prepare us to go and do by the Spirit of the Lord.

> What God had for us to do is very simple, it's not complicated. The complication is what we do with it. If we yield to Him, we too, will receive the revelation of Jesus Christ. You see, it's not just receiving it, it's the Lord preparing us that He is going to do something through us out there.

III. WE'RE LIVING IN THE DAY OF THE FULLNESS OF CHRIST

My heart was being stirred by the Word of God. I believe **God wants to give us everything** and I don't believe He wants to hold back anything. What I see in the Word, many people don't see, and maybe they see a lot of things I don't see.

One thing I see is the revelation of Jesus Christ, when he said to His disciples, "Tarry ye until you be endowed with power from on high". It was then that he gave us the Holy Ghost and fire. He also gave us the gifts and the ministry of the Holy Spirit. But the Word says that the gifts were by measure. There's also another part where He said,

> *"The Spirit of the Lord is upon me and the Spirit of wisdom..."*

> ISAIAH 11:2

What He is saying is that He wants us to have **Jesus in us so He can fulfill everything through us that the father sent Him to do – with no limitations.** We can have His Spirit without measure. We're living in that day of the fullness of time, in the fullness of the father, and that's what Ezekiel 1 is talking about.

> The full revelation of Jesus is when we lay aside our brightness, our intelligence, our everything. Those things don't matter. What really matters is that Jesus lives in us and that we receive from Him the full revelation of Jesus Christ.

The Lord told me when He brought me to the desert, "I'm going to take out of you the traditions and bondages of man. I'm going to teach you My ways." and then this is what He gave me. Ezekiel 1, 2 and 3.

We're living in the day of the fullness of Christ, the fullness of the father, in the fullness of time. We're going to allow Him to reveal Himself as he revealed Himself to Ezekiel – in the glory of the Lord, the awesomeness of His presence, and in the fullness of God. So we can go to heaven? No. There is a purpose, but God didn't give it to them. He gave it to us. Why? Because He has a plan for us. This plan is to take this Gospel of the revelation of Jesus Christ in the fullness of time, in the fullness of the Father, in the full plan of God in the last days. We have to allow the Lord to give us the revelation of the great and mighty Christ. **We have to be first a servant.** We have to get rid of our pride. We have to permit Him to clean us out so there's nothing there. Then the brightness of the glory of His presence will then fill our temples, and we'll be ready to go with Him.

There must be a reason why there is a wheel within a wheel. In John 17, Jesus prayed a prayer for us. It was a mighty prayer, that we might be in Him and He in us and He in the father and the Father in us. Ezekiel 1 is preparing us to fit in that place in the Lord. Jesus gave us His kingdom. What does His kingdom consist of? Love, peace, joy, righteousness, holiness. There is no law against it. Jesus said, "I give you this that you might take my love to the heathen." Sometimes you think, "Well, the heathen are going to go without God", but remember, that was not God's plan. He sent His Son into the world to redeem the whole world. The kings and the rulers of the earth decided they were not going to allow the people to know Him. I tell you, **God has a secret, and it's mighty** because it's the full revelation of Jesus Christ. When He's finished with us, if we will permit Him to do it, we're going to find something that we didn't know. He has made us as He is in this world. Then we can stand in the day of judgment, and we can boldly stand there because we're like Jesus.

He's giving us the privilege of that revelation in us so that we can ride upon the high places of the earth with him. If we obey Him, we will have it, and we will be riding in the glory of the Lord.

IV. A VISION – THE REALM OF ETERNITY

God gave me a vision. He lifted me in the Spirit and took me into the realm of eternity before time was. I was sitting in a home in India at a dinner table talking to a young man. The man parents were sitting with us and they were Catholics. I was sitting there and all at once, this young man asked me a question. He said, "Any religion is all right, if you believe in it, isn't it?" And all at once, I don't know what happened to me. I was still talking to them at the table but I do not know what I said to them, because all at once, I was experiencing something in the Heavens.

I was taken by the Lord into the realm of eternity, before the creation of man. I heard the Son discussing with the Father that He would be willing to become the Lamb that was slain before the foundation of the world. They discussed the creation of the world, the creation of man and then Jesus decided that He would go and become a little baby and become the Son of Man.

There was one thing that down through the years, I said to the Father. "Father, why do You permit the people to treat You the way they treat you?" He gave me the Word in Psalms and He said, "the children of Israel provoked Him to anger and He took away His Shekinah presence from them." He has caused His strength to go into captivity and His glory into the enemy's hands. He said, **"The time will come when I'm going to take My strength out of captivity and My glory out of the enemy's hands, and I'm going to show the world who I am."**

As I was witnessing these things in the heavens, I saw the **heart of God, the Father**, and I saw the price that He paid to let His beloved Son come to be cursed, blasphemed and die for a people who didn't want Him. I felt the heartbreak of the Father. I felt the heaviness, and I felt the great love of God that He had for His Son. How difficult it must have been. I think that's why it says in John,

> *"For God so loved the world, that He gave His only begotten Son that whosoever believeth in Him should not perish but have everlasting life."*

> JOHN 3:16

After the Lord had shown me this, He said, "I will not hold anybody guiltless who refuses my Son." I don't know what I said to this young man, but I'm sure I told him what the Lord said. I didn't know what had gone on at the table so I turned to my friend and I asked, "Tell me, what did I say?" She said, "I don't know, but it was wonderful."

To this day, I don't know what I said at that table that day, but the glory of the Lord was over me. It was a little difficult coming down to that table and among the people because my heart cried out, "Father, You know how much You love Your Son." We talk about how much Jesus loves us but the Father also went through a lot of things for us to have His Son. Now we're receiving the revelation of His Son.

This same Jesus became the Son of Man that He might draw us unto Himself, that we might have Him revealed to us, so that He can use us. He said, "Greater things than these shall you do because I go to My Father." You see, we're living in the end of time. We're living in the fullness of time, in the fullness of the Father. Jesus is getting us ready for the mighty flowing forth of His glory, the glory of the Lord, Jesus the Son of Man.

V. GOD IS TRANSFORMING OUR LIVES

When Ezekiel received the revelation of Jesus Christ, from that moment forward He went in the power of the Spirit. He never went in His own power. He never went thinking He was doing something. He went knowing that God was moving and speaking through him. He went knowing that it was Jesus moving and speaking through him. It is not who we are, it is the revelation of Jesus.

Remember, we're living in a day others have longed to live in, but consider who we are. We're not anybody, and yet He's going into the prisons, He's going into the streets, He's going among the gangs, He's going to transform our lives by the revelation of Himself, by the Spirit of the Lord.

Then He's going to make us mighty men and women of God because we're going to arise in the fullness of the Spirit. After he received the revelation of Jesus Christ, Ezekiel never did anything **except that he moved by the Spirit of the Lord.**

It's very important for us to allow God to change us so that we can be filled with His Spirit - the way He wants us to be. We are no match for these things. In 2 Peter, Chapter 1, we see how God is processing our life to make us as He is, filling us with His love, so that His love through us reaches out to a dying world. Read it in the King James Version as other versions leave this revelation out.

2 Peter 1 is the changing of our life into His likeness and into His nature. I believe when we get into the realm of completeness in Him, the wisdom of God is just going to flow through us, the knowledge of God is just going to flow through us and the understanding of God is just going to flow through us. How can we be in God and in Christ, and Christ in us, and not know anything about God? He is going to have charge over us so we can move by His Spirit.

He told me when He gave me the revelation of Isaiah 58 that He allowed men to acquire riches, and when He told them where to put it, they would put it there. He's given people hidden riches in the secret places. He's given them inventions. He's given them all kinds of things for this hour by the hand of God. He kept it from the world, and He's given it to those that move by His Spirit in Ezekiel 1.

Jesus said,

> *"Come unto me, all ye that labor and are heavy laden and I will give you rest. Take my yoke upon you and learn of Me, for My yoke is easy and My burden is light."*

MATTHEW 11:28

We can fly away, but we're flying in the hour of Ezekiel's wheel by the Spirit of the Lord. I trust this has dropped in your hearts. We don't have much time, but Jesus has a plan. He'll clean us up quickly, and He'll reveal Himself quickly. He'll change our lives.

Now, Jesus says, you're ready to run. You'll move when I move, and when I don't move, you don't move – you let your wings down and you rest. When He's ready to move, get ready to move. We move with Him. We don't get anxious because we've been trained by Him through the gifts, through the ministry; and, more importantly we've been trained by the Spirit of the Living God.

It was the Spirit of the Living God that was upon Ezekiel and He, today, has called us to have the Spirit of the Lord upon us.

I feel the awesomeness of what God has planned for us if we will permit Him to change our life. We will see Him as Ezekiel saw Him, then we will know that wherever the Spirit goes, that we're going to go; and when the Spirit doesn't go, we're not going to go. We're going to rest in Him. The work is mighty. Jesus in us, us in Jesus, in the middle of the wheel. We're living in the hour that God wants to use every one of us by the full revelation of Jesus Christ – **that we might ride in Ezekiel's wheel with Him.**

VI. WE HAVE THE PRIVILEGE TO WALK

Then shalt thou delight thyself in the Lord; and I
will cause thee to ride upon the high places of
the earth, and feed thee with the heritage of
Jacob thy father: for the mouth of the Lord
hath spoken it.

ISAIAH 58:14

We don't need anything else... He spoke to Ezekiel, "Son of Man, go and give them the revelation of Jesus Christ." Give it to them that they may take it to the ends of the earth.

Everything looks to the contrary, but it's not. If we will permit Him to remove from our life everything that is not of God, then His Spirit shall have the rule and reign in our life. Just as surely as this is written, it will come to pass for you.

I believe that when we come into what God has for us through the revelation of Jesus Christ that God the Father is in us and Jesus is in us and we're in them. Then we can draw our resources from heaven. We can draw our knowledge from Him. It's not our knowledge. I don't want any knowledge – all I want is God's knowledge; and when He wants me to know something; and when He wants me to have His wisdom, I want it. When He wants me to have His understanding, I want it. When He wants me to have His direction or His counsel, I want it. **This is exactly what Ezekiel's wheel is - God moving in us and us moving in Him.**

If we will permit Him to remove from our life everything that is not of God, then His Spirit shall have the rule and reign in our life. Just as surely as this is written, it will come to pass for you.

We have Jesus in the revelation of His Spirit, in the fullness of time, in the fullness of the father and in the fullness of His kingdom. How can we turn that aside? How can we choose our own greatness and try to figure everything out with our wisdom? He has it all for us, when He's ready to give it to us. Not when we're ready to take it, because we probably wouldn't have the wisdom to handle it right.

Isaiah 11:1-6

> *And there shall come forth a rod out of the stem of Jesse, and a Branch shall grow out of his roots: 2 And the spirit of the Lord shall rest upon him, the spirit of wisdom and understanding, the spirit of counsel and might, the spirit of knowledge and of the fear of the Lord; 3 And shall make him of quick understanding in the fear of the Lord: and he shall not judge after the sight of his eyes, neither reprove after the hearing of his ears:*
> *4 But with righteousness shall he judge the poor, and reprove with equity for the meek of the earth: and he shall smite the earth: with the rod of his mouth, and with the breath of his lips shall he slay the wicked. 5 And righteousness shall be the girdle of his loins, and faithfulness the girdle of his reins.*

> *6 The wolf also shall dwell with the lamb, and the leopard shall lie down with the kid; and the calf and the young lion and the fatling together; and a little child shall lead them.*

ISAIAH 11:1-6

Isaiah 11:10-11

> *10 And in that day there shall be a root of Jesse, which shall stand for an ensign of the people; to it shall the Gentiles seek: and His rest shall be glorious. 11 And it shall come to pass in that day, that the Lord shall set His hand again the second time to recover the remnant of His people, which shall be left, from Assyria, and from Egypt, and from Pathros, and from Cush, and from Elam and from Shinar, and from Hamath, and from the islands of the sea.*

ISAIAH 11:10-11

That's what God is doing today, isn't it? **He has a work to be done by us,** by the full revelation of Jesus Christ. I'm glad for the Spirit of the Lord. It is by His Spirit that He wants us to receive His Word as it is written. Today, we have the privilege to have everything that the Father gave to Jesus - and to walk in it. **Jesus came as the Son of Man, but He left us as the King of Glory.** He fulfilled everything that the Father gave Him to do that we might be filled with the fullness of the Father.

He said, "I set before you a door that no man can close". We're living in that hour – but it has to be God's way. We have to allow Him to do everything quickly so he can send us to do this work which He's called us to do.

I firmly believe the Lord wants to use the nationals in their own countries, quickly, mightily, to minister to the people by the Spirit of the Lord. **Let's remember Ezekiel could do nothing until he received the revelation of Jesus Christ.** Everywhere he went, everything he did, was by the Spirit of the Lord.

We're believing God. He's greater than all the powers of Satan. He's a mighty God, and we need to let Jesus have His way, by His Spirit, and **not to try to do it our way.** God is preparing us for a mighty work in Him. Now it has begun. It's already started. We need to prepare ourselves to move in the fullness of His Spirit to obey Him, that we might enjoy the fullness of the Father in our life – so that He can do the mighty works. We can't say what those works are because they're past our understanding. We're going to marvel as it comes, knowing that it is God. Amen.

> **Let's remember Ezekiel could do nothing until he received the revelation of Jesus Christ.**

- Rev. Agnes I. Numer

A STUDY OF THE FOUR FACES
A RIDE IN EZEKIEL'S WHEEL

Using the four Gospels to study the four faces in Ezekiel's Wheel, to see the characters and attributes of Jesus Christ that we need to have to ride in the wheel.

MARK - FACE OF THE OX
THE SERVANT

We look through Mark's Gospel at what Jesus did as a servant. Servants perform duties for others, making sure that other's needs are taken care of before their own.

The ox was considered a beast of burden. Often a yoke was put on the ox so that large loads could be carried or pulled by them.

In this study we are preparing ourselves with the attributes of a servant so that we can move with the Spirit in the wheel:

- Preparation
- Discernment
- Obedience
- Do Not Become Religious
- Who is Family
- Hearing
- Trusting
- Have Faith
- Rest

- Compassion
- Servant Heart
- Forgive
- Love
- Giving
- Watch and Pray
- Don't Follow the Crowd
- Become as the Master

PREPARATION

> *"And in the morning, rising up a great while*
> *before day, he went out, and departed into a*
> *solitary place, and there prayed."*

MARK 1:35

Servants prepare ahead of time often a 'great while' before others. This preparation of serving with God requires the attribute of prayer so that we can know the direction of the Master (God) to move with Him in the wheel.

DISCERNMENT

> *"5 When Jesus saw their faith, he said unto the*
> *sick of the palsy, Son, thy sins be forgiven*
> *thee. 6 But there were certain of the scribes*
> *sitting there, and reasoning in their hearts, 7*
> *Why doth this man thus speak blasphemies?*
> *who can forgive sins but God only? 8 And*
> *immediately when Jesus perceived in his*

spirit that they so reasoned within
themselves, he said unto them, Why reason
ye these things in your hearts? 9 Whether is
it easier to say to the sick of the palsy, Thy
sins be forgiven thee; or to say, Arise, and
take up thy bed, and walk? 10 But that ye
may know that the Son of man hath power
on earth to forgive sins, (he saith to the sick
of the palsy,) 11 I say unto thee, Arise, and
take up thy bed, and go thy way into thine
house."

MARK 2: 5-11

Jesus heard from the master that the paralyzed man needed to know first of all that his sins were forgiven. This is what was preventing him from walking. In V8 Jesus also discerns (perceived) in his spirit that there were questions in the hearts of the scribes. Because of the discernment he was able to bring healing to the paralyzed man causing him to fully recover and also correctly answer the scribes.

OBEDIENCE

Mark 2: 14-17 Jesus calls Levi (a tax collector) to be a disciple and then has a meal at his home with other publicans and sinners. The Scribes and the Pharisees question why he eats with them. The wheel was moving to show a Pharisee the truth about God. Jesus obeyed the moving of the wheel despite the religious separation. Jesus answers their question V17 "The sick needed a physician and sinners to be called to repentance".

Servants obey the master even when it is into unknown territory.

DO NOT BECOME RELIGIOUS

And Jesus said unto them, "Can the children of the
bride chamber fast, while the bridegroom is
with them? as long as they have the
bridegroom with them, they cannot fast.

MARK 2:19

Servants cannot become ridged in how they do things (become religious). Servants (disciples) obey the direction of the Master (Father) for each situation. Jesus obeyed His Father's heart, He moved by the Spirit in the wheel.

Mark 2: 27 And he said unto them, The sabbath was made for man, and not man for the sabbath: 28 Therefore the Son of man is Lord also of the sabbath.

WHO IS THE FAMILY?

31 There came then his brethren and his mother,
and, standing without, sent unto him, calling
him. 32 And the multitude sat about him,
and they said unto him, Behold, thy mother
and thy brethren without seek for thee. 33
And he answered them, saying, Who is my
mother, or my brethren? 34 And he looked
round about on them which sat about him,

and said, Behold my mother and my
brethren!

MARK 3:31-34

In this passage Jesus is expanding our thoughts and actions as a servant. Jesus did not reject his mother and brethren, but uses the opportunity to illustrate who is family. V35 "For whosoever shall do the will of God, the same is my brother, and my sister, and mother". A servant does not get to choose his family. As servants we serve those who our Father has put before us to minister to.

HEARING

"And he said unto them, Take heed what ye hear:
with what measure ye mete, it shall be
measured to you: and unto you that hear shall
more be given".

MARK 4:24

Is your heart receptive to hearing? The parable of the sower is looking at the receptiveness to the word of God. Servants must become very attuned to God's voice to be able to respond with accuracy to what the master has spoken.

TRUSTING

26 And he said, So is the kingdom of God, as if a
man should cast seed into the ground; 27 and

should sleep, and rise night and day, and the
seed should spring and grow up, he knoweth
not how. 28 For the earth bringeth forth fruit
of herself; first the blade, then the ear, after
that the full corn in the ear. 29 But when the
fruit is brought forth, immediately he putteth
in the sickle, because the harvest is come.

MARK 4: 26-29

Sow and wait for the harvest then harvest immediately ... This is the kingdom. Trust in the sower that the fruit will come forth at the right time. We only need to wait for the maturity, then immediately harvest the completed fruit.

We only need to wait for the maturity, then immediately harvest the completed fruit.

HAVE FAITH

And he said unto them, "Why are ye so fearful?
How is it that ye have no faith?"

MARK 4: 40

The storm was not concerning Jesus, but the disciples were terrified. As servants we need to have faith in where the spirit leads us in the wheel. Jesus said to go over to the other side. If he is in the boat, they should surely get there despite the very strong storm.

So often we get moving in the direction we are to go, knowing and believing it is the direction to move in with the Lord in the boat (Wheel). On the way there is a storm, or a problem that terrifies us. Are we going to give up or go back or are we going to go to the other side?

Do we trust that we have heard, and have faith that we will get through the storm?

REST

> *"And he said unto them, 'Come ye yourselves apart into a desert place, and rest a while: for there were many coming and going; and they had no leisure so much as to eat'"*

> MARK 6:31

In chapter 6 Jesus sent His disciples out with instructions to do what He had taught them.

> *And they went out, and preached that men should repent. 13 And they cast out many devils, and anointed with oil many that were sick, and healed them.*

> MARK 6:12

They also had to bury John the Baptist. Jesus himself tells them 'to come apart and rest.'

Ezekiel 1:21 'when the spirit moved they moved, when those stood they stood.'

Rest is important, we must rest when the Spirit rests.

LET'S REVIEW:

Take some time to look at the Attributes of a servant that you have already studied. **Preparation** - have you purposed to pray, so that your **Discernment** will be true? Are you **Obeying** the leading of the Spirit of the Lord? Are you moving in the wheel with **Grace** and **Truth** (righteousness), not just following the law? Your **Family**-does it encompass those that God has sent you to serve? Are you **Hearing** so that God can **Trust** you with His Harvest? Are you **Increasing in Faith** that the Spirit is leading you in the right direction? Are you learning to **Rest** when the 'wheel' stands still?

Allow the Lord to develop these servant attributes in your life so that you can move by the Spirit in the wheel. Don't just check [✓] each one off like a list. Don't file them away and think that you have passed a test.

> "Whithersoever the spirit was to go, they went,
> thither was their spirit to go; and the wheels
> were lifted up against them: for the spirit of
> the living creature was in the wheel. When
> those went, these went; and when those stood,
> these stood; and when those were lifted up
> from the earth, the wheels were lifted up
> against them, for the spirit of the living
> creature was in the wheels."

EZEKIEL 1:20-21

These servant attributes are what we need to be able to move in the Spirit in the wheel. It is a continuing work in our lives.

The late Rev. Agnes Numer would say when teaching on Ezekiel's Wheel, *"Get ready for the ride of your life."*

"Get ready for the ride of your life."

NOTES:

Before continuing, please read: Ezekiel Chapters 2 & 3

COMPASSION

We have learned about REST. Servants need to rest when the Spirit rests (in the wheel). Jesus and his disciples got in a boat to get away from the people to rest. THEN....

> *"And Jesus, when he came out, saw much people, and was **moved with compassion** toward them, because they were as sheep not having a shepherd: and he began to teach them many things."*

> MARK 6:34

This is the nitty gritty of 'wheel' life. God's timing is not our timing. His main interest is to attend to the wellbeing of His children.

At times compassion will move, and rest needs to wait, because the circumstances cannot wait. V35-44 you will see that Jesus not only taught them spiritually, but provided food for them also.

Notice that Jesus taught the whole day, this was not just a short time of 'extra' serving. Remember 'Ezekiel 1:20, 21 'When those went, these went; and when those stood, these stood..."

Note: This attribute of compassion is perhaps the turning point from just being a servant to being a 'servant son'. Denying ones' self and obedience can be self-sacrificial - we can accomplish them by ourselves perhaps - but, when we have the attribute of compassion and move on it, this is when we choose the Father's heart and we become Sons.

SERVANT HEART

> *31 And he began to teach them, that the Son of man must suffer many things, and be rejected of the elders, and of the chief priests, and scribes, and be killed, and after three days rise again. 32 And he spake that saying openly. And Peter took him, and began to rebuke him. 33 But when he had turned about and looked on his disciples, he rebuked Peter, saying, Get thee behind me, Satan: for thou savourest not the things that be of God, but the things that be of men.*

> *34 And when he had called the people unto him with his disciples also, he said unto them, Whosoever will come after me, let him deny himself, and take up his cross, and follow me. 35 For whosoever will save his life shall lose it; but whosoever shall lose his life for my sake and the gospel's, the same shall save it. 36 For what shall it profit a man, if he shall gain the whole world, and lose his own soul? 37 Or what shall a man give in exchange for his soul? 38 Whosoever therefore shall be ashamed of me and of my words in this adulterous and sinful generation; of him also*

> *shall the Son of man be ashamed, when he*
> *cometh in the glory of his Father with the holy*
> *angels.*

MARK 8:31-38

> *6 not with eyeservice, as menpleasers; but as the*
> *servants of Christ, doing the will of God from*
> *the heart; 7 with good will doing service, as to*
> *the Lord, and not to men:*

EPHESIANS 6:6-7

A servant has to be obedient to his purpose in life. An ox carries burdens for others without question and the ox does not get to consider its own needs.

Jesus explains to the people His purpose on earth. V31b "...the Son of man must suffer many things, and be rejected of the elders, and of the chief priests, and scribes, and be killed, and after three days rise again." When Peter's rebukes him, Jesus's response is V33b "For thou savourest not the things of God, but the things that are of men."

Mark 9:33-35 and 10:42-45. The dispute on who will be first and then Jesus response.

> *33 And he came to Capernaum: and being in the*
> *house he asked them, What was it that ye*
> *disputed among yourselves by the way? 34*
> *But they held their peace: for by the way they*
> *had disputed among themselves, who should*
> *be the greatest. 35 And he sat down, and*

called the twelve, and saith unto them, If any man desire to be first, the same shall be last of all, and servant of all.

MARK 9:33-35

42 But Jesus called them to him, and saith unto them, Ye know that they which are accounted to rule over the Gentiles exercise lordship over them; and their great ones exercise authority upon them. 43But so shall it not be among you: but whosoever will be great among you, shall be your minister: 44 and whosoever of you will be the chiefest, shall be servant of all. 45 For even the Son of man came not to be ministered unto, but to minister, and to give his life a ransom for many.

MARK 10:42-45

In 9:35 "And he sat down and called the twelve, and saith unto them, If any man desire to be first, the same shall be last of all, and servant of all." Also in 10:45 "For even the Son of man came not to be ministered unto, but to minister, and to give his life a ransom for many."

FORGIVE

As a burden bearer (the ox), the servant can be subject to overuse. This happens when we serve in our own strength and we do not move when the spirit moves. This can cause us to be angry and bitter which can lead to unforgiveness.

25 And when ye stand praying, forgive, if ye have ought against any: that your Father also which is in heaven may forgive you your trespasses. 26 But if ye do not forgive, neither will your Father which is in heaven forgive your trespasses.

MARK 11:25-26

We need to forgive so we can be free to move in the majestic wheel.

LOVE

Mark 12:28-31. A scribe asks Jesus this question - what is the first commandment of all? Jesus's reply is

29 And Jesus answered him, The first of all the commandments is , Hear, O Israel; The Lord our God is one Lord: 30 and thou shalt love the Lord thy God with all thy heart, and with all thy soul, and with all thy mind, and with all thy strength: this is the first commandment. 31 And the second is like, namely this, Thou shalt love thy neighbour as thyself. There is none other commandment greater than these.

MARK 12:29-31

The scribe responds in 12:33

33 and to love him with all the heart, and with all
the understanding, and with all the soul, and
with all the strength, and to love his
neighbour as himself, is more than all whole
burnt offerings and sacrifices.

MARK 12:33

To love the Lord our God with ALL our soul, and our neighbour with ALL/AS ourselves, would make the WHOLE burnt offering. This would be acceptable to the Lord, a 'sweet smell'.

The whole is: All of the heart, All of the soul, All of the mind, and All of the strength. This is the Love of a servant to the Master.

GIVING

43 And he called unto him *his disciples, and saith*
unto them, Verily I say unto you, That this
poor widow hath cast more in, than all they
which have cast into the treasury: 44 for all
they did cast in of their abundance; but she of
her want did cast in all that she had, even all
her living.

MARK 12: 43-44

The widow gave all that she could. A servant's giving is

sacrificial. Are you giving out of your abundance or out of your need?

WATCH AND PRAY

> *34* For the Son of man is *as a man taking a far*
> *journey, who left his house, and gave*
> *authority to his servants, and to every man*
> *his work, and commanded the porter to*
> *watch. 35 Watch ye therefore: for ye know not*
> *when the master of the house cometh, at even,*
> *or at midnight, or at the cockcrowing, or in the*
> *morning: 36 lest coming suddenly he find you*
> *sleeping. 37And what I say unto you I say*
> *unto all, Watch.*

MARK 13: 34- 37

The Master goes on a journey and gives Authority to his servants, and to every man a job or work to do and commanded the porter to watch. V35"Watch ye therefore: for ye know not when the master of the house cometh, at even or at midnight, or at the cock crowing, or in the morning."

"Watch and pray lest you enter into temptation, the spirit truly is ready, but the flesh is weak."

Work keeps us busy and about our Master's business.

Watching for the master's return keeps us alert to the future. Watching and Praying keeps us from entering into temptation.

These are attributes that transform us from servant to son.

DON'T FOLLOW THE CROWD.

3 And being in Bethany in the house of Simon the leper, as he sat at meat, there came a woman having an alabaster box of ointment of spikenard very precious; and she break the box, and poured it on his head. 4 And there were some that had indignation within themselves, and said, Why was this waste of the ointment made? 5 For it might have been sold for more than three hundred pence, and have been given to the poor. And they murmured against her. 6 And Jesus said, Let her alone; why trouble ye her? She hath wrought a good work on me. 7 For ye have the poor with you always, and whensoever ye will ye may do them good: but me ye have not always. 8 She hath done what she could: she is come aforehand to anoint my body to the burying. 9 Verily I say unto you, Wheresoever this gospel shall be preached throughout the whole world, this also that she hath done shall be spoken of for a memorial of her.

MARK 14:3-9

Our focus is on the wellbeing of people. Jesus was visiting an outcast, Simon the leper, and a woman was anointing Him with expensive oil that others watching thought could have been used for a more noble purpose, like feeding the poor.

Helping people find salvation into God's kingdom is what is more important than what the crowd thinks or how people are showing their gratitude.

Be guided by the Spirit moving in the wheel rather than the traditions of man. Become more aware of where the Spirit is moving and go where He is going.

Moving with the Spirit is not always with a crowd or majority.

For a further study on the Beatitudes, read the book "Journey to the Rock: The Climb", by All Nations International.

LET'S REVIEW

Take time again to reflect and pray on which of these attributes of a servant need to become greater in your life. Remember this is getting ready so that you can move with Jesus in the wheel. With **Compassion** Jesus was able to continue to minster to the crowd despite His need to rest. This is **a wheel schedule!** A word of caution here, turn back to the first four attributes: **Preparation, Discernment, Obedience,** and **Do Not Become Religious.** These four, and maybe others, should have a firm foundation in us otherwise the "doing" of compassion might become a "good work" which will not produce life for you, or those being ministered to.

How about a servant heart? We continue to see that **servant** is all about others. Then we come to **forgiving.** It will be difficult to ride the wheel with unforgiveness riding on your back. Take a look at the beatitudes (read Matthew 5:1-12) as part of the study. There are many similarities there. So when you are ready to go on, look at the attribute of **love.** A full sacrifice is to love God and others. This is an acceptable sacrifice. You might be on this section for a while. Don't rush. Again, I remind you, this is to be part of the "wheel life". We continue to giving, sacrificial giving.

And then, let us **not** miss **watch and pray.** Yes, servants need to watch and pray so that we are not led into temptation.

NOTES:

BECOME AS THE MASTER

> *15 And he said unto them, "Go ye into all the*
> *world, and preach the gospel to every*
> *creature. 16 He that believeth and is baptized*
> *shall be saved; but he that believeth not shall*
> *be damned; 17 And these signs shall follow*
> *them that believe; in my name shall they cast*
> *out devils; they shall speak with new tongues;*
> *18 They shall take up serpents; and if they*
> *drink any deadly thing, it shall not hurt them;*
> *they shall lay hands on the sick, and they*
> *shall recover.*
>
> MARK 16:15-18

As we take on the attributes of a servant, we learn the master's ways. We learn to see the needs of others and with willingness serve them.

We will then be Sons of God, able to move with the Spirit in the wheel.

We will move when the Spirit moves, and rest when He rests, and it will be the greatest ride of our lives!

> *And they went every one straight forward: whither the*
> *spirit was to go.*
>
> EZEKIEL 1:12

JOHN - FACE OF THE EAGLE

SON OF GOD

Eagles are strong birds of prey. They protect and nourish their young. They can see very far. They also encourage and guide their young into maturity.

In John's Gospel we look at the attributes of Jesus as the Son of God, the Eagle, his nature, strength, obedience and trust. And his father so that he could fulfill his destiny.

The purpose of this study is to develop the attributes of a Son of God. To mature and acknowledge who we are in God, so that we can move in that authority in the 'wheel' with the Spirit of God.

We will look through John's Gospel at what Jesus did as the Son of God. The Nature of the Son, His mission and His understanding of who He was... the Son of the most High God.

ATTRIBUTES OF A SON OF GOD

- Receive him
- Born Again
- Grace and truth
- Zeal for the home
- Obedience
- Believe
- Have righteous judgment
- Continue in the word
- Abide in the House
- Work while it is Day
- Give your life
- Serve with Love
- Be Fruitful & love
- Ask
- Speak Openly
- Fulfill your purpose - Son of God

RECEIVE HIM

> *4 In him was life and the life was the light of men.
> 9 That was the true light which lighteth every
> man that cometh into the world. 12 But as
> many as received him, to them gave he power
> to become the sons of God, even to them that
> believe on his name:*

> JOHN 1:4, 9, 12

BORN AGAIN

> 5 *Jesus answered, "Truly, truly, I say to you,*
> *unless one is born of water and the Spirit he*
> *cannot enter into the kingdom of God. 6 "That*
> *which is born of the flesh is flesh, and that*
> *which is born of the Spirit is spirit. 7 "Do not*
> *be amazed that I said to you, 'You must be*
> *born again.'*

JOHN 3:5-7

> 16 *For God so loved the world that he gave his*
> *only begotten Son, that whosoever believeth in*
> *him should not perish, but have everlasting*
> *life.*

JOHN 3:16

Our new birth gives us the capacity not to condemn, but through our lives bring people to salvation. Being a Son of God.

Before we look at the attributes and functions of a son of God we must receive him as Lord and believe on His name. It is only then that we get the power and ability to take on the attributes and be sons. Have your received Jesus Christ into your life as Lord and Savior? Are you a son? You must receive Him as Lord of your life, to have power and ability to become complete sons.

GRACE AND TRUTH

> *17 For the law was given by Moses, but grace and*
> *truth came by Jesus Christ.*

JOHN 1:17

Grace means unmerited divine assistance.

Truth means the real or true facts about something.

Christ came to fulfill the Law of Moses by grace and truth. Grace and Truth by Jesus Christ (direction from the Father) must become an integral attribute of our character. This is a principal foundation of being a son.

Grace and Truth is the fulfillment of the Law.

ZEAL FOR THE HOUSE

> *17 And he said unto them that sold doves, "Take*
> *these things hence; make not my Father's*
> *house a house of merchandise." And his*
> *disciples remembered that it is written, "The*
> *zeal of thine house has eaten me up."*

JOHN 2:16, 17

God's house should be kept sanctified? This house is not only the building of worship, but also our living temple that we have invited God to live in- ourselves.

If our house is not filled with the righteousness of the Father we will not be able to see clearly when the Spirit is moving in the wheel. We will be blinded because our house is not pure.

As sons we need to be jealous for the Holiness of God's house.

OBEDIENCE

> *34 My meat is to do the will of him that sent me,*
> *and to finish (complete) his work.*

JOHN 4:34

Jesus obeyed his father's leading by speaking to this Samaritan woman and thereby bringing her whole village to God's saving grace.

> *17 My Father worketh hitherto, and I work.*

JOHN 5:17

This statement comes after Jesus heals the lame man at the pool on the sabbath. The Jews want to kill him because it is not the law to work on the sabbath.

> *19 Verily, verily, I say unto you, The Son can do*
> *nothing of himself; but what he seeth the*
> *Father do: for what things so ever he doeth,*
> *these also doeth the Son likewise.*

JOHN 5:19

*30 I can of mine own self do nothing: as I hear, I
judge: and my judgement is just; because I
seek not mine own will, but the will of my
Father which hath sent me.*

JOHN 5:30

When moving in the wheel, obedience is a key. We are learning Kingdom ways that are not man's ways. Imagine being led by the Spirit of the Lord, "wheel moving", in a similar circumstance like speaking to the Samaritan woman at the well?

Maturity is also necessary along with obedience, so we can be trusted with situations similar to this. Develop the attribute of obedience, so that you can move in the wheel by God's Grace and Truth. Obedience is not bondage - it is the Son's good pleasure to obey the Father. Joy, comfort and satisfaction are the reward when we move with our Father in the 'wheel'.

Note: Obedience is also a **servant** attribute.

BELIEVE

*"Jesus answered them and said, "Most assuredly, I
am sent to you, you are seeking me, not
because you saw attesting miracles, but
because you ate of the loaves and were
satisfyingly filled. Stop working for the food*

which perishes, but work for the food which
abides for life eternal which the Son of Man
will give you, for this One the Father sealed,
even God." Then they said to him, "what are
we to do as a habit of life that we may
continually be working the works of God?"
Answered Jesus and said to them, "This is the
work of God that you continually be believing
on Him whom that One sent off on a mission."

JOHN 6:26-29 WUEST
TRANSLATION

Sons - continue to Believe in your Father God.

HAVE RIGHTEOUS JUDGEMENT

24 Judge not according to the appearance, but
judge righteous judgment.

JOHN 7:24

Jesus responded to those who were angry about him healing on the Sabbath. Here is a great lesson on moving in the wheel: A man needed to be healed that hour, just as a boy needed to be circumcised on the eighth day, but according to law, one should not work on the Sabbath. As sons, by Grace and Truth, it is also righteous to heal those who are sick or cast down or oppressed by the devil.

Remember Jesus did not come to take away the law but to fulfill it.

LET'S REVIEW:

Have you received Jesus as Lord and Savior? Have you been Born again of Water (been water baptized) **and** of the **Spirit** (received the Holy Spirit with evidence of speaking in your heavenly language)? Do you have **Grace and Truth** operating in you? Has your **Zeal for God's house** increased? Are you being **obedient** to His will? Are you **believing** your Father? And is **Grace and Truth** helping you make **Righteous Judgment?**

You might have to **stop for a while** and do some **housekeeping.** Many of us get born again and just continue walking along the same road we've been on. This could work for a short time but we need a new tunic and outer-coat. It requires putting off the old man and putting on the new man. Remember, when you receive Him as Lord, He gives you the power to become a son of God. This is a continuing process.

> *28b I do nothing of myself but as my Father hath*
> *taught me I speak these things. 29 And he that*
> *sent me is with me: the Father hath not left me*
> *alone; for I do always those things which*
> *please him.*

JOHN 8:28B-29

With this encouragement let us continue to look at St. John's Gospel in this light of seeing the attributes which will make us mature sons of God - to be able to move in the 'Wheel'.

NOTES:

CONTINUE IN THE WORD

31Then said Jesus to those Jews which believed on
him, if ye continue in my word, then are you
my disciples indeed; 32 and ye shall know the
truth, and the truth shall make you free.

JOHN 8:31-32

We need to continue studying the Word as disciplined sons. We will then know the truth and the truth will set us free. Truth here is God's divine revelation - this is freedom! A son needs to know how his father works, therefore we have to know our Father, spend time with Him, work with Him, and discuss things with Him. In other words, read the manual - the word of God, and phone the manufacturer - pray.

ABIDE IN THE HOUSE

34 Verily, verily, I say unto you, whosoever
committeth sin is the servant of sin. 35And the
servant abideth not in the house for ever: but
the Son abideth forever.

JOHN 8:34-35

Abide means to accept or act in accordance with a rule, decision or recommendation. Once we have accepted to be the sons of God, we need to 'abide' forever in His house.

We need to abide forever in His house.

WORK WHILE IT IS DAY

> *4 I must work the works of him that sent me,*
>   *while it is day: the night cometh, when no*
>   *man can work. 5 As long as I am in the world,*
>   *I am the light of the world.*

JOHN 9:4-5

A son needs to be about his father's business while it is day, while there is still the light of God. Understand that our life in Christ is a life time experience and that it is continuous until Christ comes for us. We are the light of the world, and we have to take every opportunity to share this with others so that they can come to God's saving grace.

GIVE YOUR LIFE:

> *11 I am the good shepherd: the good shepherd,*
>   *giveth his life for the sheep.*
> *John 10:11*

Jesus refers to himself as the 'good shepherd' laying his life down for all sheep who know and hear His voice. As a son we need to protect the people of God, not allowing the devil to steal, kill and destroy the flock. Hirelings allow the 'sheep' to be scattered and killed. Sons care for their household, making sure all are safe and accounted for.

SERVE WITH LOVE

Jesus set a standard here washing his disciple's feet. So profound washing his disciple's feet.

> *13 He said to them, do you understand what I*
> *have done to you? You call me the teacher and*
> *the Lord and well do you say for I Am. 14*
> *Since therefore I, the Lord and Teacher,*
> *washed your feet, you also have a moral*
> *obligation to be washing one another's feet, for*
> *I gave to you an example that just as I did to*
> *you, you also should be doing.*
>
> JOHN 13:13-14

> *In this all shall know that you are my disciples if*
> *you constantly have love among one another.*
>
> JOHN 13:35 WUEST
> TRANSLATION

As sons of God our heritage is great, we should understand that we are no greater than those who serve.

BE FRUITFUL AND LOVE

> *I appointed you in order that you might be going*
> *away and constantly bearing fruit, and that*
> *your fruit might be remaining, in order that*
> *whatever you might ask the Father in my*

*name, He may give it to you. These things I
am enjoining upon you namely that you
should be loving one another with a divine
and sacrificial love.*

JOHN 15:16-17 WUEST
TRANSLATION

Being fruitful requires us to do something. It requires a living communion with Jesus as the true vine, it also requires sacrificial love for the brethren - bearing fruit.

ASK

*24 Hitherto have ye asked nothing in my name:
ask, and ye shall receive, that your joy may be
full.*

JOHN16:24

Several times Jesus talks to his disciples about asking of the father. It is the prerogative of sons to ask their fathers for things, even with abandon (without holding back). Jesus says ask and ye shall receive. In our world today, we might have a wrong understanding of asking for things from our Father. As a Father, are you encouraging your children to ask things from you? And do you have the attributes of your Father God to be able to give your children the 'good' things? Let's develop the attributes of our heavenly Father so that our children can ask, and we give because we have. This is "wheel" living.

SPEAK OPENLY

Then the chief priest asked Jesus concerning his disciples and concerning His teaching Jesus answered him, as for myself, I have spoken openly to the world. I at all times taught in the synagogue and in the temple where all the Jews habitually come together, and in secret I said nothing.

JOHN: 18:19-20 WUEST TRANSLATION

Jesus says some amazing things that we need to take note of. He says. "I spake openly **to the world.**" So he spoke to all. Then he says "I ever taught **in the synagogue**," (this is to the local church) "and **in the temple**, whither the Jews always resort;" (**the greater congregation** went to hear teaching and to talk about doctrine) "and in secret have I said nothing". Jesus had no hidden agenda, He spoke to everyone. What he spoke and discussed was always the truth, we as sons of God should have this same attribute in all that we do and say.

FULFILL YOUR PURPOSE – SON OF GOD

The disciples go fishing, their former (previous) occupation. They catch nothing. In the morning Jesus appeared on the shore and enquires. "Boys still under instruction, you do not have anything to add to your bread, such as fish, have you?" John 21:5. Jesus directs them to throw their nets on the right side, they catch a very full net, and the net does not break. Jesus already has fish on the fire when they come to shore. Jesus says. V10 "Bring at once some of the fish you have now caught." Then V12 "here have some breakfast." They eat together and afterwards Jesus asks Peter V15, 16, and 17. "Do you love me more than these [fish]?" Peter's reply is yes all three times. Jesus's instruction is "Be feeding my little lambs, be shepherding my sheep, be feeding my sheep."

Sometimes we go back to our old job (lifestyle), we lose direction, and we become discouraged.

Jesus's encouragement: -

- He enquires about 'the catch'
- He instructs them on where the fish are.
- He provides some fish
- He invites them to bring some of the fish that they have caught.
- They enjoy the meal together, bread and fish.
- Then Jesus helps Peter affirm (declare) his love for Jesus - Peter's new occupation over the previous occupation of 'fishing'.
- Jesus encourages Peter again to feed and take care of the flock.

Let us attain the attributes of a son of God, and let us continue to mature, for the purpose of Moving with the Spirit in the wheel to 'be shepherding the sheep'.

"Be feeding my little lambs, be shepherding my sheep, be feeding my sheep."

Jesus's last instruction to Peter was: **Follow me.**

LET'S REVIEW

Continue in the Word - intimacy and knowledge in God's ways is what matures us.

Abide - Stay in God. Abide means to accept and act in accordance with a rule, decision and recommendation. Operating under this guidance, there is great security.

Work while it is day - this is true "wheel" life. "Day" is when the Spirit is moving. Remember in Mark, the Servant, the attribute compassion? Even though there was a need to rest, the people had no shepherd and Jesus rose up with compassion and moved to help them. This is similar to **"give your life"**. Laying one's own life down for the sheep. We also have to **humbly serve** our brethren. Do not forget to **ask** your Father, Who gives you good things, He is your Father God.

To move in the wheel as a "Son of God" requires following God.

~

It's time to ride.

NOTES:

LUKE - FACE OF MAN
SON OF MAN

We look through Luke's Gospel at attributes that are needed to be a son of man. We look at Jesus' example in his humanity, how He lived on earth among men. How he did things, what he had to work through, his obedience and his acceptance of his destiny. We will learn how to live as a man on earth.

Enjoy, learn and accept your destiny.

ATTRIBUTES OF THE SON OF MAN

- Accept Your Destiny
- Let Others Acknowledge You
- Prophetic Confirmation
- Study to be Called
- Obey the Law of God and Land
- Do Not Fear or Reject Trials
- Move in the Authority
- Martha and Mary

- Occupy
- Seek the Kingdom - First
- Compassion
- Count the Cost
- Watch and Pray
- Be Endued (Filled) with Power

ACCEPT YOUR DESTINY

We read in Luke 1:26-37, the Angel Gabriel was sent by God to tell Mary she would conceive, and be the mother of Jesus. Here we see the call of God on Mary's life. The angel came to speak directly to Mary about her destiny, even though Mary was troubled, and fearful she willingly accepted this 'call'.

> *38 And Mary said, 'Behold the handmaid of the*
> *Lord; be it unto me according to thy word'.*

LUKE 1:38

It is important to note that because of Mary's acceptance of the call on her life that it was possible for Jesus to be born. We want to hear from our Maker and accept His desire for our lives to fulfill His purpose on earth. If we are not fully invested in our destiny we will find it very difficult to move in the wheel - it will be in our own strength.

Let us desire to move in the wheel and fulfill God's purpose for our lives. Can you say as Mary said, "Be it unto me, according to thy word?"

"Be it unto me, according to thy word."

LET OTHERS ACKNOWLEDGE YOU

We read in Luke 1:39-48 when Mary comes to visit Elizabeth, John leapt in Elizabeth's womb, acknowledging Jesus. The spirit in Elizabeth acknowledges Mary and Jesus.

> *42 And she spake out with a loud voice, and said,*
> *Blessed art thou among woman, and blessed is*
> *the fruit of thy womb.*

> LUKE 1:42

The Holy Spirit moved through Elizabeth, and the baby John leaped in her womb V45 Elizabeth says "And blessed is she that believed: for there shall be a performance of those things which were told her from the Lord." The acknowledgement is of Mary's believing, and her willingness, that the Lord will fulfill destiny through her.

Mary responds:

> *46 And Mary said, my soul doth magnify the*
> *Lord, 47 and my spirit hath rejoiced in God*
> *my Saviour. 48 For he hath regarded the low*
> *estate of his handmaiden:"*

> LUKE 1:46-48

Mary acknowledges the Lord's call upon her and expresses humility. Are you secure in your destiny? Can you wait for the acknowledgement from others?

PROPHETIC CONFIRMATION

Read Luke 2:25-38. When Jesus was brought to the temple to be dedicated by his parents, both Simeon, a devout man who was promised by God that he would not die until he saw the Christ, and Anna the prophetess witnessed that Jesus was the one to come (the Messiah).

Prophetic acknowledgement:

1. It confirms our destiny, what we are called to be.
2. It declares our calling to others.

Note: be careful that you let the Holy Spirit do the acknowledging. God is the one who knows when the time is right.

STUDY TO BE CALLED

> *40 And the child grew, and waxed strong in spirit, filled with wisdom: and the grace of God was upon him.*

LUKE 2:40

> *52 And Jesus increased in wisdom and stature, and in favour with man and God.*

LUKE 2:52

Jesus learned natural skills from Joseph, (his trade as a carpenter,) and he also went to the local Synagogue (church) and learned the foundation principles of his faith. Jesus went to Jerusalem and spent time with the scholars which added knowledge and helped mature him.

To be the son of man we have to know our heritage, our calling and we have to know how to live.

OBEY THE LAW OF GOD AND THE LAND

> *21 Now when all the people were baptized, it came to pass that Jesus also being baptized, and praying, the heaven was opened, 22 and the Holy Ghost descended in a bodily shape like a dove upon him, and a voice came from heaven, which said, Thou are my beloved Son; in t I am well pleased.*

> LUKE 3:21-22

Baptism is to confirm our faith in God and to declare who we belong to. Jesus's Father acknowledges this commitment also declaring that Jesus is His Son. Jesus was obedient to both His Father and the law.

DO NOT FEAR OR REJECT TRIALS

Read Luke 4: 1-13. Jesus is led into the wilderness by the Holy Spirit. He ate nothing, and He was tempted by the devil for 40 days. The devil challenged Jesus, but because He knew who He was, He responded with the word and authority to the temptation of the devil. Trials help to strengthen us and confirm our position (calling).

After this experience...Jesus went to the synagogue and was given the book of Isaiah to read, he reads from chapter 61:1-2.

> *1 The spirit of the Lord God is upon me; because the Lord hath anointed me to preach good tidings (the gospel) unto the meek; he hath sent me to bind up the brokenhearted, to proclaim liberty to the captives, and the opening of the prison to them that are bound; 2 To proclaim the acceptable year of the Lord.*

ISAIAH 61:1-2

Jesus just confirmed His calling.

LET'S REVIEW:

In preparing to move with the Spirit in the wheel as the son of man, we have looked at the following attributes:

To first, **become a son.** Then **accept your destiny, let others acknowledge you, get prophetic confirmation, study** to be called, **obey the law** of God and the land, **do not fear or reject trials,** this will mature you.

When we move with the Spirit in the wheel, we want to have attributes that will help our fellow man. Our confidence of who we are as sons needs to be sure. We cannot be overcome by doubts, fears, or insecurities when on a mission.

Jesus could not have read from the scriptures and declared who He was with confidence without the encouragement from parents, mentors, teachers, and prophets. He also spent time studying the scriptures, (the word of God).

In the wheel we have to focus on the task at hand, in tune with what the Spirit in the wheel is doing.

What do you look like right now as the son of man? Are you taking on His attributes? Are you taking the right steps in your walk in becoming a son of man? Are you following God's plans to fulfill your destiny?

Many aspects of being a Son of man are similar to the attributes of being a 'Son of God'. While this may seem repetitive, the main point for Luke's Gospel is to have attributes to effectively work with man. Remember, we are maturing to move with the Spirit in the wheel.

NOTES:

MOVE IN THE AUTHORITY

Luke 4:32 "And they were astonished at his doctrine: for his word was with power." When we teach, are others astonished at our doctrine? Is there authority in our words? When Jesus taught His word was with power. Consider your life, what situations might you face where you will need this authority?

Do you understand the authority that you have as the son of man? Here are just a few that were highlighted for me.

We have authority over:

- Demons - Luke 4:33-35
- Disease - Luke 4:38, 39
- Nature Luke: 5:1-11. Although Simon was a fisherman by trade he obeyed when Jesus instructed him to go into the deep and let down the net. Do we trust and obey in the same way even though it is contrary to our natural instincts?
- Defilement Luke 5:12-14 The leper required more than a healing. His circumstance called for a cleansing.
- Laws Luke 6:1- Remember Jesus came to fulfill the law. Laws are not meant to bind us or confine - they are meant to free (liberate) us. The religious leaders were addressing the law of not working on the Sabbath. Jesus responds by referring them to the law about gleaning Duet. 23:25

9 Whom shall he teach knowledge? And whom
shall he make to understand doctrine? Them

*that are weaned from the milk, and drawn
from the breast. 10 For precept must be upon
precept, precept upon precept; line upon line,
line upon line; here a little, and there a little:*

ISAIAH 28:9-10

*47 Whosoever cometh to me, and heareth my
sayings, and doeth them, I will show you to
whom he is like: 48 he is like a man who build
an house and digged deep, and laid the
foundation on the rock: and when the flood
arose, the stream beat vehemently on the
house, and could not shake it: for it was
founded on a rock. 49 But he that heareth and
doeth not, is like a man that without a
foundation built a house upon the earth:
against which the stream beat vehemently
and immediately it fell; and the ruin of that
house was great.*

LUKE 6:47-49

The compassion to man is very evident in Luke's Gospel. These are some of the things that we as sons do when moving in the wheel.

- Heal the Sick (Luke 7:8-10) Jesus was willing to go to a centurion's house to heal his servant and even at the end not go into the house.
- Raise the Dead (Luke 7:11-15) The only motivation

was compassion, not for any other reason. There does not need to be a reason to do something good.

- Testimony and Actions to Remove Doubt. (Luke 7:18-23) Jesus did not rebuke John or his disciples for wanting reassurance, he continued doing what he came to earth to do thus giving them the assurance.

No pride should come at this point. In humbleness always do what you have been anointed and called to do. Jesus was just doing what he was meant to do. So often we try to make a bigger demonstration, do something extravagant. Why?

And then what did Jesus do?

Jesus only did what He saw the Father do.

- Acknowledge others (Luke 7:24-29) Jesus speaks of John and acknowledges him. Jesus quickly disannulled the doubt that people might have had towards John for asking such a question. Let us be quick to acknowledge and authenticate our brothers and sisters.
- Give Wise Counsel (Luke 7:36-50) Jesus goes to Simon's house to eat and there also the woman washes his feet with oil. Oh to get to that place in God where we can without offense use opportunities to give wise council.
- Feed the hungry (Luke 9:10-17) Noticing when people need to have food and extending oneself to feed them.
- Follow the Father's will (Luke 9:22-26) For sons to be

able to move in the wheel and to be effective, our Father's priority comes first.

For the Son of man is not come to destroy men's lives, but to save them. Luke 9:56

MARTHA AND MARY

Read Luke 10: 38. Jesus was at Martha and Mary's house visiting them. It says Martha was encumbered about much serving and was getting overwhelmed. Mary, on the other hand, was at Jesus's feet and this was where the Spirit was moving. Martha also had to be there, but had to provide food.

> *But Martha was going around in circles, over-occupied with preparing the meal. And bursting in upon Jesus she assumed a stance over Him and said, "Lord, is it not a concern to you that my sister has let me down to be preparing the meal alone? Speak therefore to her at once that she take hold and do her part with me." And answering, the Lord said to her, "Martha, Martha, you are worried and excited about many things, but of few things there is need, or of one, for Mary chose out for herself the good portion, which is of such a nature that it shall not hastily be snatched away from her.*

> MATTHEW 10: 40-42 WUEST TRANSLATION

What activities are you doing that are not necessary (over occupied) and might cause you to miss where the Spirit is going and 'miss' the ride in the wheel because we were 'encumbered with'...?

OCCUPY

> When the unclean spirit is gone out of a man, he
>   walketh through dry places, seeking rest: and
>   finding none, he sayeth I will return unto my
>   house whence I came out. 25 And when he
>   cometh, he findeth it swept and garnished. 26
>   Then goeth he and taketh to him seven other
>   spirits more wicked than himself; and they
>   enter in and dwell there: and the last state of
>   the man is worse than the first.
>
> LUKE 11:24-26

When your house has been swept clean, what clean things, God things, must you put into your new "son of man" house? It will not be good just to sweep and decorate. Take time to think what must occupy the cleaned house. Let the Lord show what gaps are in your Christian foundation and occupy.

SEEK THE KINGDOM - FIRST

Read Luke 12:14-34. What a great world we could live in if we could grasp this concept and have it working in our lives? V23. "The life is more than meat, and the body is more than raiment". Apply this to your life and let God show you what this really means to you. I think this is a very difficult area to give to our Father and have trust enough that He will fully provide for us. V29 "And seek not what ye shall eat, or what ye shall drink, neither be ye of a doubtful mind." How often do we doubt the Father's provision for us? There are several situations in Luke's Gospel where he looks at trusting the Father. How can we overcome in these areas? V31 and 32 shows us how to do this.

> *31 But rather seek ye the kingdom of God; and all these things shall be added unto you. 32 Fear not, little flock; for it is your Father's good pleasure to give you the Kingdom.*

> LUKE 12:31-32

Do you see this? It is the Father's good pleasure, **His good pleasure!!** Son of man, where is your treasure?

> *34 For where your treasure is, there will your heart be also.*

> LUKE 12:34

Purpose in yourself to 'let God' and experience the incredible freedom of 'all things' being added to you.

COMPASSION

> *8 And he answering said unto him, Lord, let it*

alone this year also, till I shall dig about it,
and dung it: 9 and if it bear fruit, well; and if
not, then after that thou shall cut it down.

LUKE 13:8-9

Compassion often requires us to spend our extra time with people to give them a chance to bear fruit.

COUNT THE COST

Read Luke 14:25-35.

Being a son of man has a price, but there is security, contentment, peace and joy when we fully embrace this. But, we do need to count the cost, because it does take work and commitment to be a son.

Read Luke 15: 11-32. The familiar passage about the prodigal son. This son realized the security in being part of his father's house, he was even prepared to be a servant in the household. Also look at the older son's anger, but most importantly see the father's response.

31 And he said unto him, Son, thou art ever with
me, and all that I have is thine.

LUKE 15:31

Do you realize what is yours as sons?

29 And he said unto them, Verily I say unto you,
There is a no man that hath left house, or

parents, or brethren, or wife, or children, for
the kingdom of God's sake, 30Who shall not
receive manifold more in this present time,
and in the time to come life everlasting.

LUKE 18:29-30

10 For the Son of man is come to seek and to save
that which was lost."

LUKE 19:10

LET'S REVIEW:

Remember that the reason for this study is to move in the wheel when the SPIRIT moves, to minister to man on earth. Embrace all that is a Son so that you can bring those who are lost to salvation?

MOVING IN AUTHORITY OVER...

Remember authority comes from being with and learning from the Father. It is **'His Authority'.**

Martha or Mary. Have you discovered where you belong? Is it time to serve or to sit? Pay attention to where the Spirit is and position yourself there, don't be busy doing unnecessary things.

Are you **occupying** and filling yourself with what will make you a son? **Seeking** the Kingdom? How about **compassion?** Have you **counted the cost** of being a son? Are you fully invested?

NOTES:

WATCH AND PRAY

> *And take heed to yourselves, lest at any time your hearts be overcharged with surfeiting, and drunkenness, and cares of this life, and so that day come upon you unawares. Watch ye therefore, and pray always, that ye may be accounted worthy to escape all these things that shall come to pass, and to stand before the Son of man. But be circumspect, attentive, ready, in every season being in prayer, in order that you may have sufficient strength to be escaping all these things which are about to take place, and to stand before the son of man.*

> LUKE 21:34-36 WUEST
> TRANSLATION

What love had Jesus for His brothers to continually warn, but most importantly encourage them to watch and pray so that they would not be overcome by the enemy. We need to continually watch and pray.

BE ENDUED WITH POWER

> *49 And, behold, I send the promise of my Father upon you: but tarry ye in the city of Jerusalem, until ye be endued with power from on high.*

> LUKE 24:49

Sons, do you have the power from on high? We must have all the attributes of the Son to be the sons of man. Will you tarry in the city until you be endued with power from on high? Are you in for the long haul, will you wait until you have been endued? Then you truly will have the ability to move by the Spirit in the wheel.

Wait to be endued with power of the Holy Spirit,
So we can ride in the wheel.

MATTHEW - FACE OF THE LION

JESUS THE KING - HIS AUTHORITY

Matthews's Gospel is written for God's chosen people, the Jews, the Tribe of Judah. In this book our focus is to see how we 'God's Chosen' can come into a greater understanding of Kingdom Living, through the knowledge of our heritage, because of the life that Jesus lived and demonstrated for us. We will also look at some other people who demonstrated effectual living as believers.

WHAT ATTRIBUTES DO WE NEED TO HAVE AND EMBRACE TO MOVE WITH THE SPIRIT OF GOD IN THE WHEEL AS GOD'S CHOSEN PEOPLE?

- Ordinary man
- Wise Man
- Appointed Man
- Obedience
- Knowledge

- Fulfilling the Law
- Living the Kingdom Way
- Proof of Kingdom Life
- Be Planted
- A Pure Heart
- Do not be Deceived
- Savour the Things of God
- Prayer and Fasting
- Preparation
- Faithful
- Wise
- Break Bread Together
- Know Your Destiny

ORDINARY MAN

> 20 But while he thought on these things, behold,
> the angel of the Lord appeared unto him in a
> dream, saying, Joseph, thou son of David, fear
> not to take unto thee Mary thy wife: for that
> which is conceived in her is of the Holy Ghost.
> 21 And she shall bring forth a son, and thou
> shalt call his name JESUS: for he shall save
> his people from their sins. 22 Now all this was
> done, that it might be fulfilled which was
> spoken of the Lord by the prophet, saying, 23
> Behold, a virgin shall be with child, and shall
> bring forth a son, And they shall call his name
> Emmanuel, which being interpreted is, God
> with us. 24 Then Joseph being raised from

sleep did as the angel of the Lord had bidden
him, and took unto him his wife:

MATTHEW 1:20-24

Joseph is directed by an angel of the Lord to take Mary as his
wife. Joseph did as the angel of the Lord bid him and he
called the child's name Jesus when he was born. Joseph was
a carpenter, an ordinary person? Yes just a carpenter. Yet
Joseph had a conversation with an angel, knew that it was
from God, believed the messenger and was willing to obey.
What kind of a man was he? Just an ordinary man, a son of
David. He was not only willing to take Mary as his wife,
bearing the shame that she was already pregnant, but chose
to believe the messenger from God and to allow 'History' to
unfold. V25 "And knew her not till she had brought forth her
firstborn son: and he (Joseph) called his name JESUS."

It was the 'norm' in that time to live a life that was governed
by the law (Moses law). Joseph was not a priest, nor a
Pharisee, nor an evangelist. He was an ordinary man living
an ordinary life, a carpenter.

WISE MAN

1 "Now when Jesus was born in Bethlehem of
Judea in the days of Herod the King, behold,
there came wise men from the east to
Jerusalem, 2 saying, where is he that is born
King of the Jews? For we have seen his star in
the east, and are come to worship him."

MATTHEW 2:1-2

These wise men (magis) were learned men especially in the study of the stars, they also would have had to have historical knowledge to know about the Christ. Because of their wisdom and knowledge they had followed the star to come and worship the new King. Unlike Herod's scholars who read the scriptures but were not wise to understand their meaning.

Knowledge of history and what has been foretold is an essential part of being able to move in the wheel. As God's chosen we need to get ourselves in position by knowing our (Christian) history, our past and our future. This requires diligent study. "Why should we do these things" you say? - So when the wheel begins to move we are prepared and we can go where the spirit is moving with the wheel, just like the wise men.

It does not only take knowledge by learning, but a heart that is after the things of God.

APPOINTED MAN

*13 'Then cometh Jesus from Galilee to Jordan unto John, to be baptized of him. 14 But John forbad him, saying, I have need to be baptized of thee, and comest thou to me? 15 And Jesus, answering said unto him, suffer it to be so now: for thus it becometh us to **fulfill all righteousness**. Then he suffered him.'*

MATTHEW 3:13-15

Both Jesus and John were appointed men, appointed for a specific job.

We see Jesus here determined to fulfill all righteousness, and John consents to the request. Jesus was the son of God. He did not need to be baptized, yet He did this to fulfill all righteousness, and make history.

LET'S REVIEW:

Are you living an **ordinary** believer's life? Could you, by your ordinary life as a Christian, be in 'line' to have an **extraordinary** appointment? Like Joseph, Mary or even Elizabeth? Are you a **wise man**, knowing the times and positioning yourself to be in the right place to witness history being made—like the wise men, or even Simeon and Anna? Are you an **appointed man** moving forward in righteousness to complete the job you have been appointed to do, like John and Jesus?

Know your destiny so you can fulfill it and not be derailed.

We will now look at the attributes that you will need to enable you to accomplish this.

NOTES:

OBEDIENCE

> *12 "And being warned of God in a dream that they should not return to Herod, they departed into their own country another way. 13b "And when they were departed, behold, the angel of the Lord appeared to Joseph in a dream, saying, Arise, and take the child and his mother, and flee into Egypt, and be there until I bring thee word...14 when he arose he took the young child and his mother by night, and departed into Egypt"*

MATTHEW 2:12, 13B, 14

The obedience was without question. The child, Jesus, would have been murdered if the wise men had not gone a different way. Joseph would not have had time to escape to Egypt if he had waited. If Jesus and John had not obeyed the law to baptize Jesus the confirmation by the Spirit, that Jesus was the son of God could not have happened.

Obedience is an attribute of God's chosen people that is necessary to be able to move in the wheel. Ezekiel 1:12

KNOWLEDGE

Our knowledge of our foundation and biblical history is so important. It gives us a stepping stone into our future. The truths from what was said and done can direct our steps. Let's look at how Jesus used historical truth after his wilderness experience when the devil tempted him.

4 "But he answered and said, It is written, Man shall not live by bread alone, but by every word that proceedeth out of the mouth of God."

MATTHEW 4:4

As a young boy, Jesus would have studied the books of the law. Deuteronomy 8:3c reads: "....that he might make thee know that man doth not live by bread only, but by every word that proceedeth out of the mouth of the Lord doth man live." In Matthew 4:7 Jesus responds: "It is written again, Thou shalt not tempt the Lord your God" (Deuteronomy 6:16) Matthew 4:10 "Then saith Jesus unto him, Get thee hence, Satan; for it is written, Thou shalt worship the Lord thy God, and him only shalt thou serve". Deuteronomy 10:20 "Thou shalt fear the Lord thy God; him shalt thou serve, and to him halt thou cleave, and swear by his name."

Jesus was able, with the knowledge of the Law (His foundation), to make a firm declaration against Satan's temptation using the word of God. Satan knew the word of God, he was unable to argue with Jesus. The word is truth and power.

Read Deuteronomy 6:12-20. This will give you much insight into the reason we as believers need our history.

FULFILLING THE LAW

Read Matthew 5:1-16. Jesus is teaching His disciples principles of living, through foundational truths, encouraging the disciples to apply themselves. Then in

Matthew 5:17-20, He firmly states that as children of God we need to keep all the law plus love righteousness, the righteousness that fulfills the law.

We are looking at a lifestyle – wholly acceptable to God.

> 20 *"For I say unto you, that except your righteousness shall exceed the righteousness of the scribes and Pharisees, ye shall in no case enter into the kingdom of heaven."*

MATTHEW 5:20

This passage is important to understand, and apply to our lives. It is key to successful ministry to the family of Christ. Jesus assures the disciples that the mosaic laws were still applicable, but righteousness (grace and truth) need to be applied to fulfill the law.

As a believer, a member of the body of Christ, is your righteousness 'exceeding?'

Matthew 5:19b says "but whomever shall do and teach the same shall be called great in the kingdom of heaven." Assess before God where you are in your life, in obtaining these attributes of a true believer. It does not matter what you do, it matters what type of righteousness you have (the law or the law with grace and truth). Jesus did not come to destroy the law He came to fulfill it.

Do you know the foundation principles of the Christian faith?

What does the foundation mean to you?

Our heritage, our history, and our foundation is what makes us who we are. Joseph the father of Jesus, the Wise men, John the Baptist and Jesus knew the foundation of their faith. They were taught as young children at the Synagogue, at the family table every week, and on remembrance days like Passover. This learning and foundation is what enabled them to live their lives to the full and make history.

They listened, they studied, they obeyed and they used the knowledge of their heritage to fulfill their destiny.

LIVING THE KINGDOM WAY

Read Matthew chapters 5 – 7. You will see Jesus teaching on various aspects of kingdom living using the laws written in Exodus, Leviticus, Deuteronomy and Judges. He gives insight to these situations so that the law is not a ritual, but governed by righteousness (grace and mercy) so that there is liberty.

What ways are you still living by the letter of the law? Begin to learn and live by righteous application so that you can move with the Spirit in the wheel. We must 'Come up higher in God's Love' to move in the wheel.

Some examples of the Law and Kingdom thinking.

- The law - If you kill you will be judged. Matthew 5:21
- Kingdom Thinking - If you are angry and say Raca,

or say someone is a fool, you will be in danger of
going to hell. Matthew 5:22

- The law- Do not commit adultery. Matthew 5:27
- Kingdom Thinking- Wuest 'Everyone who is
  looking at a woman in order to indulge his sexual
  passion for her, already committed adultery with
  her in his heart.' Matthew 5:28

- The law-Don't take an oath on yourself ...or of the
  Lord because it is binding. Matthew 5:33
- Kingdom Thinking - Don't take an oath by anything
  or anyone. Let your communication be yea, yea or
  nay, nay. Matthew 5:34, 37

- The Law- 'Love thy Neighbor, hate thine enemy.'
  Matthew 5:43
- Kingdom Thinking- 'Love your enemy, bless those
  who curse you, do good to those who hate you, and
  pray for them which despitefully use you, and
  persecute you.' Matthew 5:44

- The religion- When doing alms they sound a
  trumpet. Matthew 6:1
- The righteousness- Do your alms in secret, let your
  father in heaven reward you. Matthew 6:3, 4

- The Religion- 'Hypocrites pray standing in the
  synagogue and at the street corners.' Matthew 6:5
- The Righteousness- 'Enter into thy closet, pray in
  secret to your Father, who will reward you openly'
  Matthew 6:6

16' And, behold, one came and said unto him,
Good Master, what good thing shall I do, that
I may have eternal life? 17 And he said unto
him, Why callest thou me good? there is none
good but one, that is, God: but if thou wilt
enter into life, keep the commandments. 18 He
saith unto him, Which? Jesus said, Thou shalt
do no murder, Thou shalt not commit
adultery, Thou shalt not steal, Thou shalt not
bear false witness, 19 Honour thy father and
thy mother: and, Thou shalt love thy
neighbour as thyself. 20 The young man saith
unto him, All these things have I kept from
my youth up: what lack I yet? 21 Jesus said
unto him, If thou wilt be perfect, go and sell
that thou hast, and give to the poor, and thou
shalt have treasure in heaven: and come and
follow me. 22 But when the young man heard
that saying, he went away sorrowful: for he
had great possessions. 23 Then said Jesus unto
his disciples, Verily I say unto you, That a
rich man shall hardly enter into the kingdom
of heaven.'

MATTHEW 19:16-23

Jesus was not being unkind to the young man, he was addressing the heart attitude of the man. Wuest translation helps us understand what Jesus was saying "But Jesus says to him, Start following with me as my disciple and continue to do so as a habit of life...," When we make things habits in our lives, this is when there will be fruit, good or bad. Our goal in this study is to make our 'habit of life' the Kingdom Life - this is what produces fruit, good fruit, so we can ride in the wheel with the Spirit of God.

Allow God to show you the areas in your life that need to be fulfilled and righteous. As you begin to make these attributes habits in your life, it will become so natural, you will begin to move with the Spirit in the wheel without thinking about it.

PROOF OF KINGDOM LIFE

16 "Ye shall know them by their fruits. Do men gather grapes of thorns, or figs of thistles?"

MATTHEW 7:16

18 "A good tree cannot bring forth evil fruit, neither can a corrupt tree bring forth good fruit."

MATTHEW 7:18

21 "Not everyone that saith unto me, Lord, Lord, shall enter into the kingdom of heaven; but he that doeth the will of my Father which is in heaven."

MATTHEW 7:21

37 "Then saith he unto his disciples, The harvest truly is plenteous, but the labourers are few;

38 pray ye therefore the Lord of the harvest,
that he will send forth labourers into the
harvest."

MATTHEW 9:37,38

We are looking at what we produce that comes from the result of being mature sons of the Kingdom of God. The reason is to move in the wheel with the Spirit of the Lord to...

- Heal - The leper asks 'if thou wilt, thou canst make me clean.' ...Jesus puts forth his hand and says 'I will, be thou clean.' To bring healing is a product of kingdom living. Matthew 8:3, 4, 5
- Cast out Demons- The authority we have by the 'word' enables us to speak to these spirits and they will obey the word. Matthew 8:28-33
- Have Authority - The well-known story of the centurion... "I am not worthy that thou shouldest come under my roof: but speak the word only, and my servant shall be healed. For I am a man under authority, having soldiers under me: and I say to this man go and he goeth...." The centurion recognized that Jesus was under authority. Matthew 8:8
- Have Mercy - Remember that we are being sent to the lost, those that need a physician. Matthew 9:12, 13
- Go to the lost sheep of Israel- Matthew 10:6
- Declare that the kingdom of heaven is at hand- Matthew 10:7
- Raise the dead - Matthew 10:8

"Then said he unto his disciples, The Harvest truly is plenteous, but the labourers are few; Pray ye therefore the Lord of the harvest, that he will send forth labourers, into the harvest." Matthew 9:37, 38

BE PLANTED

Read Matthew 13:24-30, 37-43.

We so often get caught up in worrying about the wickedness around us that we try to stop it and get uprooted ourselves. As sons of the kingdom we need to be about our Father's business, doing what He has appointed us to do - be planted, grow in God and bear fruit. When the harvest is ready our Father in heaven will come for us, and welcome us home and those who were sown as deception will be condemned.

What does this have to do with the moving in the wheel? We need to spend more time growing and maturing to produce good fruit to be part of the good harvest and not contend with the evil that is being sown. Let us be determined to be planted of God. In Matthew 13:14 Jesus says 'let them alone....' We can often spend valuable time trying to destroy evil around us, debating and arguing. It is our job to mature, bear fruit and move with the Spirit in the wheel so that there can be a harvest.

God is the one who will separate the fruit from the tares when He returns.

A PURE HEART

> *18 "But those things which proceed out of the mouth come forth from the heart; and they defile the man."*

MATTHEW 15:18

Law is good - this keeps us safe - but if our hearts are not washed with the word, what we partake of (take into our heart and spirit man) will defile us and that is what will come out of our hearts.

LET'S REVIEW

Matthew's Gospel looks at the Kingship authority. **Obedience** is a key attribute. We also have obedience as an attribute in Mark's Gospel - the servant. The Magi obeyed God. Joseph obeyed God. Jesus Himself obeyed His Father God. Who do you obey? A voice of God, the Holy Spirit? So, you have to get to know the voice of God to be able to hear and obey. We need **knowledge** of our foundation so we can move in our kingdom authority as Jesus did speaking truth to the devil. Now comes the completeness, fulfilling the law. This is also linked with obedience and knowledge. Now, Jesus teaches and shows us true kingdom lifestyle, applying the law with **truth** and **grace**. As we apply and embrace these key attributes, how maturing it will be so we can alway live the kingdom way. We must "come up higher" in order to lead others to the Lord. So let's purpose to be **firmly planted** in Christ. You will mature and grow and be part of the harvest. And be sure to wash yourselves in the word to have a **pure heart.**

Becoming kingdom sons requires us to wash ourselves in the Word, take on His attributes, and live a lifestyle that reveals who we belong to—the Tribe of Judah.

NOTES:

DO NOT BE DECEIVED

Read Matthew 16: 1-12.

The religious leaders were tempting Jesus, asking for a sign from heaven. He cautions his disciples to not be blinded by the (false) teaching of the Pharisees and Sadducees, the religiousness of their teaching.

SAVOUR THE THINGS OF GOD

In Matthew 16 we read:

> 21 *"From that time forth began Jesus to shew unto his disciples, how that he must go unto Jerusalem, and suffer many things of the elders and chief priests and scribes, and be killed, and be raised again the third day."*

MATTHEW 16:21

When Peter rebukes him, Jesus's response is:

> 23 *"Get thee behind me, Satan: thou art an offence unto me: for thou **savourest** not the things that be of God, but those that be of men."*

MATTHEW 16:23

Jesus knew his destiny, therefore he was able to purpose to fulfill it. Imagine what would have happened if Jesus had got out of the wheel at that point?

PRAYER AND FASTING

> 21 *"Howbeit this kind goeth not out but by prayer and fasting."*

MATTHEW 17:21

This particular response comes after the disciples are not able to rebuke the devil out of a child, Jesus said the disciples were of 'little faith' The attribute of praying and fasting is what increases faith and what is necessary for certain 'kinds' of demonic forces. Remember we are looking at attributes of the Kingdom in Matthews's Gospel so that we can move in the wheel to serve our family, the body of Christ.

Let us look at some of the functions we might need to have to serve the body of Christ.

> 25 *"But Jesus called them unto him, and said, 'Ye know that the princes of the Gentiles exercise dominion over them, and they that are great exercise authority upon them. 26 But it shall not be so among you: whosoever will be great among you, let him be your minister; 27 and whosoever will be chief among you, let him be your servant; 28 even as the Son of man came not to be ministered unto, but to minister, and to give his life a ransom for many.'"*

MATTHEW 20:25-28

Some examples from Matthew chapters 18-21:

- Take time to find the lost and rejoice - Matthew 18:13
- Correct ways to solve problems - Matthew: 18:15 -17
- Coming into agreement in His name - Matthew: 18:18-20
- Principle of forgiving - Matthew: 18. 21-35

PREPARATION

> 11 *"And when the king came in to see the guests, he saw there a man which had not on a wedding garment: 12 And he saith unto him, Friend, how camest thou in thither not having a wedding garment? And he was speechless."*
>
> MATTHEW 22:11-12

After the wedding guests were called there was still room at the banquet, because some were too busy attending to 'life'. The call to salvation is to all those who are destitute and lost, even from the highways and byways.

Jesus invites all that are lost, when we accept the invitation (of salvation), we must prepare ourselves (as a bride) for the coming of the 'bridegroom'.

FAITHFUL

> 45 *"Who then is a faithful and wise servant, whom his lord hath made ruler over his*

household, to give them meat in due season?
46 Blessed is that servant, whom his lord
when he cometh shall find so doing. 47 Verily I
say unto you, that he shall make him ruler
over all his goods."

MATTHEW 24:45-47

When the lord of the house is able to leave the responsibility of the family to a faithful and wise servant and know that his household will be taken care of, this is maturity. Faithfulness is a key attribute to moving in the wheel.

WISE

Read Matthew 25: 1-30. Righteous wisdom is also a key attribute to our goals in life. Like the examples of the wise virgins and the servants who were given talents. If we were to wait or try and help others who are not making an effort themselves, we could find ourselves not ready to be at the wedding feast or not able to reproduce what God has appointed for us to do. The result is not being able to ride in the wheel.

BREAK BREAD TOGETHER

Read Matthew 26:26-28. When we have a meal together as believers we are instructed to break bread to remember Jesus's sacrifice. This will encourage us to get the attributes that we need, that we are bonded together, and remember what the purpose of Jesus's death was for.

KNOW YOUR DESTINY

> 51 'And, behold, one of them which were with
> Jesus stretched out his hand, and drew his
> sword, and struck a servant of the high
> priest's, and smote off his ear. 52 Then said
> Jesus unto him, Put up again thy sword into
> his place: for all they that take the sword shall
> perish with the sword. 53 Thinkest thou that I
> cannot now pray to my Father, and he shall
> presently give me more than twelve legions of
> angels? 54 But how then shall the scriptures
> be fulfilled, that thus it must be?'

MATTHEW 26:51-54

It is important to fight the correct battle and not get ahead of the wheel. Jesus encourages everyone to allow the fulfillment of their destiny. "But how then shall the scriptures be fulfilled, that thus it must be."

LET'S REVIEW

Do you know your **authority**, the way Jesus knew His as Lion of the tribe of Judah? Do you have the **Word of God** in you, and **savor** the things of God, so you cannot be deceived? Are you praying and fasting? Remember that **praying and fasting** are key attributes to having His authority over the enemy. Are you **preparing** yourself for the Bridegroom? Are you **faithfully** doing what you have been called to do? Don't forget to attain **wisdom** and have fellowship and **break bread** to remember Jesus. And the last one, know your **destiny**, because without a vision, you will perish.

NOTES:

COMMISSION

This is the purpose!!!! To be commissioned. All the attributes of Christ, as the servant –the Ox, as the son of God – the Eagle, as the son of Man – the Man, and our heritage as God's chosen – the Lion is what we need to have to be able to move with God by the Spirit in the wheel, when we are commissioned.

> *19 " 'Go ye therefore, and teach all nations,*
> *baptizing them in the name of the Father, and*
> *of the Son, and of the Holy Ghost: 20 teaching*
> *them to observe all things whatsoever I have*
> *commanded you: and lo, I am with you*
> *always, even unto the end of the world.'*
> *Amen."*

MATTHEW 28:19, 20

Let Us Ride with the King to see His Kingdom Come

GLOSSARY

- **Attributes** - Fancy English word for Character
- **Character** - Dominant qualities distinguishing a person or group
- **Exalted** - Held in high esteem.
- **Revelation** - To show us something we did not know or see before.
- **Yield** - To surrender or submit oneself to another.

ABOUT THE AUTHOR

Annella Whitehead is a nurse, ordained minister, and international trainer with over 38 years in missions. She has served in Africa, Asia, and America, equipping leaders in health, agriculture, and biblical training. Based in the U.S. with All Nations International, she continues to teach  and serve globally. When Annella is not teaching, she enjoys spending time in her garden and creating delicious meals in the kitchen, combining her love for nature, creativity, and hospitality.